MARCHING TOWARD
FREEDOM

MARCHING TOWARD FREEDOM

by VIRGINIA SCHOMP

mc Marshall Cavendish
Benchmark
New York

The author and publisher are grateful to Jill Watts, professor of history
at California State University, San Marcos, for her perceptive comments on the manuscript,
and to the late Richard Newman, civil rights advocate, author, and senior research officer
at the W. E. B. DuBois Institute at Harvard University,
for his excellent work in formulating the series.

❈❈

EDITOR: JOYCE STANTON   PUBLISHER: MICHELLE BISSON
ART DIRECTOR: ANAHID HAMPARIAN   SERIES DESIGNER: MICHAEL NELSON

Photo research by Connie Gardner Cover photo by Lucien Aigner/CORBIS: Back Cover: Alinari Archives/The Image Works: Time and Life Pictures/Getty
Images; pages 1, 2-3, 33: Lawrence, Jacob (1917-2000)c ARS, NY, They also made it very difficult for migrants leaving the South. They often went to railroad sta-
tions and arrested the Negroes wholesale, which in turn made them miss their train. 1940-41. Panel 42 from The Migration Series. Tempera on gesso on composition board, 18 x 12". Gift of Mrs. David M. Levy (28.1942.21) The Museum of Modern Art, New York NY, U.S.A. Digital Image © The Museum of Modern
Art/Licensed by SCALA/Art Resource, NY; page 6: Smithsonian American Art Museum, Washington DC/Art Resource, NY; pages 6,8: Hulton Archive/Getty
Images; pages 9, 19: Bettmann/CORBIS; pages 10, 17, 26, 34, 36, 37, 41, 46, 48, 51, 55, 59, 67, 68, 71, 72, 73: Lawrence, Jacob (1917-2001) c ARS, NY, Ice Peddlers, 1936. Tempera on paper, 26 x 19 _". Private Collection, The Jacob and Gwendolyn Lawrence Foundation/Art Resource, NY; page 12: Schert/SV-Bilderdi-
enst/The Image Works; pages 13, 61: CORBIS; pages 14, 39, 57: Topham/The Image Works; pages 15, 47, 52: Arthur Siegel/CORBIS; page 18: HIP/Art
Resource, NY; page 20; Underwood and Underwood/CORBIS; pages 23, 40: Arthur Rothstein/CORBIS; page 24: Schomburg Center/Art Resource, NY; page
27: National Portrait Gallery, Smithsonian Institution/Art Resource, NY; pages 29, 60: The Granger Collection; page 30: Lawrence, Jacob (1917-2000) c ARS, NY,
One of the main forms of social and recreational activities in which the migrants indulged occurred in the church. 1940-41. Panel 52 from the Migration Series. Tempera on gesso on composition board 18 x 12". Gift of Mr. and Mrs. David M. Levy. (28.1942.27). The Museum of Modern Art, New York, NY, U.S.A. The Museum
of Modern Art/Licensed by SCALA/Art Resource, NY; page 42: Lucien Aigner/CORBIS; page 44: Lawrence, Jacob (1917-2000) c ARS, NY, Ironers,
1943.Gouache on paper, 21 1/2 x 29 1/2", Location: Private Collection, Photo, The Jacob and Gwendolyn Lawrence Foundation/Art Resource, NY; page 49: The
Everett Collection; page 50: A soldier in combat overalls using a field telephone on Saipan Island, 1944 (b/w photo) Peter Newark Military Pictures/Bridgeman Art
Library; page 62: John Vachon/CORBIS, page 64; Marion Post Wolcott/CORBIS, page 70.

A NOTE ON LANGUAGE

In order to preserve the character and historical accuracy of the quoted material appearing in this book, we
have not corrected or modernized spellings, capitalization, punctuation, or grammar. We have retained the
"dialect spelling" that was sometimes used by white writers in an attempt to reproduce the way some black
southerners spoke. You will occasionally come across outdated or offensive words, such as *colored*, *Negro*,
and *nigger*, which were often used by both white and black Americans at the turn of the twentieth century.

Front cover: Men and women cook together at a community kitchen in New York City's Harlem during the
Great Depression.
Back cover: Track-and-field champion Jesse Owens in 1935
Half-title page: Sisters Linda and Terry Lynn Brown attended a segregated school in Kansas before their parents
won the famous 1954 civil rights lawsuit *Brown* v. *Board of Education*.
Title page: A billboard portraying American prosperity makes an odd backdrop for African Americans lined up for
relief during the Great Depression.

CONTENTS

INTRODUCTION

Marching toward Freedom is the eighth volume in the series Drama of African-American History. Earlier books in this series have followed the journey of African Americans from the start of the transatlantic slave trade in the fifteenth century through the Harlem Renaissance in the early twentieth century. Now we will explore the dramatic period between 1929 and 1954—a quarter century that marked a turning point in the long, hard struggle against prejudice and discrimination.

The early years of the twentieth century had been a time of great change and optimism in the African-American community. Two million black men, women, and children had taken part in the Great Migration, moving from southern rural areas to cities in the North. Blacks left the South to escape an endless cycle of poverty, oppression, and racial violence. To many desperate migrants, the North seemed like a "promised land" of freedom and opportunity. The reality was somewhat different. Southern blacks did find plenty of jobs in northern industrial centers such as Chicago, Detroit, Philadelphia, and New York. They found that Jim Crow—the discriminatory system that created segregated public services and facilities for blacks—was not the law of the land in the North as it was in the South. But even in northern cities, African Americans were nearly always restricted to the lowest-paying jobs in labor and domestic service. They also faced continued prejudice and discrimination in housing,

Opposite: It was always not easy for blacks to leave the South during the Great Migration. They might be harassed or arrested at railroad stations and forced to miss their trains. A policeman looms threateningly large in this painting by African-American artist Jacob Lawerence.

Street Life by the celebrated Harlem Renaissance painter William H. Johnson

education, and many other areas of public life.

African Americans responded to these challenges with a renewed commitment to the battle against racism. The black soldiers who returned from service in World War I in 1919 were ready to fight back when confronted with injustice and violence at home. Black migrants, crowded in vibrant African-American communities such as Harlem in New York City, were embracing a new vision of self-respect and self-reliance. They rejected the old images of inferiority and dependence imposed on them by white Americans. In place of those negative stereotypes, they began to forge a new identity for themselves as a people. A "New Negro" emerged, proud of his or her racial heritage and determined to topple the barriers to black advancement.

The dynamic spirit of the New Negro found its finest expression in the exciting period known as the Harlem Renaissance. During the 1920s and early 1930s, Renaissance writers, artists, and musicians explored and celebrated African-American culture and achievements. They produced important novels, poetry, paintings, sculptures, and brand-new forms of music, including blues and jazz. Their works showed the world that there was no limit to the capabilities and talents of their race.

The Harlem Renaissance came to an end in the early 1930s with the start of the Great Depression. While that economic crisis affected nearly every American, blacks were hit hardest of all. They endured not only crushing poverty but also rising discrimination, racial tensions, and racial violence. At the same time, the Depression years brought a new sense of unity and self-determination to the black community. Banding together, African Americans formed political, religious, and labor organizations to work for an end to discrimination. These activists would continue their work through World War II and beyond, laying the groundwork for the modern civil rights movement.

A man joins the NAACP, the leading civil rights organization of the 1930s and 1940s.

Chapter 1

THE GREAT DEPRESSION

A middle-aged black woman, her face worn with care, stood before the desk of a city welfare worker in Pittsburgh, Pennsylvania, in 1931. The desperate woman was the mother of six children. She needed help providing for her youngsters. She had no money for food or clothing. Their home had no heat, because she could not pay the gas bills. Their landlord had threatened to evict them in five days if they did not pay their rent.

"Where is your husband?" asked the welfare worker.

"He worked in the steel mills for four-five years and was a good man," the woman explained. "The mill closed and he was laid off. He went out early every morning and walked the streets until night, looking for work. Day after day he done this ever since last June. Once a man told him that he needn't trouble looking for a job as long as there is so many white men out of work. I guess us colored folk don't get hungry like white folks. He just got discouraged

Opposite: A mother and her four children in rural Mississippi during the Great Depression

and one day he went out and didn't come back. He told me once that if he wasn't living at home the welfare people would help me and the kids, and maybe he just went away on that account."

Hanging On by a Thread

The crash of the stock market on October 29, 1929, signaled the start of the Great Depression. Within three years, nearly half of America's banks would close. Manufacturing output would fall more than 50 percent. More than 13 million Americans would lose their jobs.

Hard times were nothing new for African Americans. Even in the "boom years" before the Depression, when businesses raked in record profits and stock prices soared, hundreds of thousands of black families were barely scraping out a living on small farms in the South. Meanwhile, in the North, African Americans labored at the lowest-paying jobs in factories, coal mines, brickyards, meat-packing plants, and transit companies. When new machines began to displace unskilled laborers in the mid-1920s, black workers were the first to lose their jobs.

After the crash in 1929, employers again laid off their black workers first. Black unemployment worsened as the Depression deepened and desperate whites grabbed any job they could get—even so-called "Negro jobs" such as garbage collecting, street cleaning, and domestic service. By 1934, 38 percent of black Americans were unemployed, compared to 17 percent of

Ice Peddlers by Jacob Lawrence depicts a poor but vibrant New York City neighborhood in 1936.

whites. With little or no savings to fall back on, many black families soon became desperate for the basic necessities of life: food, clothing, shelter, medicine.

President Herbert Hoover maintained that the federal government had no business aiding the needy. Instead, he believed that public assistance should come from state and local governments and private charities. Those sources were quickly overwhelmed, however. In the early years of the Depression, only one out of every four unemployed workers was able to find relief.

As always, discrimination added to the hardships suffered by black Americans. Many state and city agencies made it especially hard for African Americans to qualify for public assistance. Needy blacks who did qualify received smaller benefits than

These shacks in a Manhattan "shantytown" were home to the homeless during the Great Depression.

whites. In Atlanta, for example, whites received an average monthly allowance of $32.66, while blacks got just $19.29. In addition, private charities and religious organizations dominated by whites often refused to provide any aid to blacks.

In February 1931 the National Urban League, a leading civil rights organization, reported that many African Americans had "given up their homes, pawned their clothes, sold their furniture and are persistently hanging on by the barest thread." Anna Arnold Hedgeman, a social worker for the Young Women's Christian Association

(YWCA) in New York City's Harlem, described "a large mass of Negroes [who] were faced with the reality of starvation. . . . [M]en, women, and children combed the streets and searched in garbage cans for food, foraging with dogs and cats."

A sharecropper picks cotton in a South Carolina farm field in 1938.

Henry Robinson lived on a small farm in the South for nineteen years. Each year the black sharecropper raised three bales of cotton and turned them over to his white landlord. Each year he fell deeper in debt. "I know we been beat out of money direct and indirect," said Robinson. "You see, they [the landowners] . . . can overcharge us and I know it's being done. I made three bales again last year. He said I owed $400 the beginning of the year. Now you can't dispute his word. When I said 'Suh?' he said 'Don't you dispute my word; the book says so.' When the book says so and so you better pay it, or they will say, 'So, I'm a liar, eh?' You better take to the bushes too if you dispute him, for he will string you up for that."

WORKING FOR THE MAN

The Great Migration had taken two million African Americans from the South to the North. Nevertheless, at the start of the Depression, four out of five African Americans still lived in southern rural areas. Most black southerners were farmers. Some worked as wage laborers, earning as little as forty to sixty-five cents a day. Many others were sharecroppers. They worked small

A plantation owner and his workers in the Mississippi Delta region, 1936. This picture was taken by the famous Depression-era photographer Dorothea Lange.

plots of land owned by white landlords, paying rent with a share of the crops they raised. Sharecroppers often had to borrow the cost of tools, seeds, fertilizer, food, clothing, and other supplies from their landlords. At the end of the year, when these advances were deducted along with the landowner's share, there was usually little or nothing left for the farmer. "Ain't make nothing, don't speck nothing no more till I die," said one black sharecropper. "We jest work for de other man. He git everything."

At the start of the Great Depression, cotton prices plummeted. Sharecroppers found it harder and harder to climb out from under their mountains of debt. At the same time, many landowners began to experiment with laborsaving devices such as mechanical cotton pickers. Operating these machines was considered a "white man's job." With no work, many black families lost their homes and farms. Little or no public assistance was available in most rural areas of the South. Some black families survived by growing what they could and supplementing their diet by hunting and fishing. Others faced a stark choice: move or starve. During the 1930s, about 400,000 southern blacks followed the path of earlier migrants who had headed north. They had little chance of finding steady jobs in the crowded northern cities. But at least there was the hope of finding some small measure of relief to get them through the terrible times.

In March 1931 two groups of boys, one black and one white, hopped aboard a freight train in Tennessee. A fight broke out, and the white boys were tossed from the car. Humiliated, they complained to the local authorities. When the sheriff stopped the train near Scottsboro, Alabama, he found nine black youths ranging in age from thirteen to twenty, along with two white girls. Hoping to avoid arrest, the girls accused the black boys of rape. Medical examinations proved that their story was false. Still, the boys were rushed to trial. An all-white jury swiftly found them guilty and condemned eight of them to death. (The youngest boy was sentenced to life imprisonment.)

The case of the "Scottsboro Boys" provoked widespread outrage. Lawyers from the International Labor Defense, a Communist organization that took up their defense, described the verdict as a "legal lynching." After many years of appeals and retrials, all of the young men were eventually set free. The last man left prison in 1950, after serving nearly twenty years for a crime he did not commit.

A REIGN OF TERROR

The case of the Scottsboro Boys was evidence of the racism deeply rooted in American society, especially in the South. More than six decades after the end of the Civil War, white southerners still insisted that the region was and always would be "a white man's country." Under the Jim Crow system, African Americans were restricted to segregated facilities and services, which were nearly always inferior to those available to whites. They were barred from voting and serving on juries. They were discriminated against in education, housing, employment, and nearly every other area of public life.

Jim Crow was enforced not only through laws but also through intimidation and violence. The crime of lynching, in which victims suspected of offenses are murdered by lawless mobs, had decreased in the 1920s. During the Great Depression,

Seven of the "Scottsboro Boys" with their attorney, Samuel Leibowitz, at an Alabama jail

White tenants put up this sign to discourage African Americans from applying for apartments in a Detroit public housing project.

racial tensions and job competition led to a resurgence of the brutal practice. There were seven reported lynchings in 1929, followed by twenty-one in each of the next three years. A report issued in 1935 by the Commission on Interracial Cooperation, a group of white and black southerners who united to combat racial violence, found that the "typical lynching is in the rural South, the mob victim is a Negro, the lynchers are native-born whites, and the courts punish no one." Despite hopes that the brutal crime would die out, the report concluded, "Lynchings are not fading nationally from the American scene; the mob still rides."

Racist whites often tried to excuse lynching by claiming that "mob justice" was needed to protect southern white women from "savage" black men. The real aim of lynching, however, was to intimidate and control blacks. Increasingly, lynchers targeted black workers and sharecroppers who stood up for their rights. One white landowner advised his sons to shoot or hang any "disrespectful" black croppers. In Atlanta unemployed whites organized the Black Shirts, a terrorist group whose slogan was "No Jobs for Niggers Until Every White Man Has a Job." In Mississippi white railroad workers murdered seven black men employed as firemen, whose job included tending and fueling locomotive engines. The firemen's only "crime" was working at a high-paying, skilled job coveted by whites. "Mississippi, in its own primitive way, had begun to deal with the unemployment problem," observed reporter Hilton Butler. "Dust had been blown from the shotgun, the whip, and the noose, and Ku Klux [Klan] practices were being resumed in the certainty that dead men not only tell no tales but create vacancies."

In 1933 the Commission on Interracial Cooperation called for federal legislation against lynching. Scores of other organizations joined the campaign, including the National Association for the Advancement of Colored People (NAACP), the American Civil Liberties Union, the International Labor Defense, the National Council of Jewish Women, the YWCA, and the Methodist Woman's Missionary Council. Despite mass rallies and increasing public support, Congress never passed an antilynching bill. However, the campaign did compel several southern states to crack down on mob violence with their own antilynching measures. The number of victims murdered by lynch mobs would drop from a peak of twenty-eight in 1933 to two in 1939. Throughout the 1930s, the antilynching crusade would also attract millions of white supporters throughout the nation to the battle for civil rights.

The NAACP hung a black flag outside its headquarters in New York City to mark each occurrence of the brutal crime of lynching.

Chapter 2

A New Deal

BY THE FALL OF 1932, A BLANKET OF GLOOM had settled over the nation. That year the Republicans nominated Herbert Hoover for a second term as president. Hoover offered no new ideas for helping the millions of needy Americans or ending the Great Depression. In his first term, he had turned a blind eye to discrimination, segregation, and lynching. Despite this dismal record, most African Americans remained loyal to the Republican Party of Abraham Lincoln and emancipation.

Black loyalty to the Republicans was partly due to the fact that the Democrats did not seem to offer anything better. The Democratic candidate for president was Franklin D. Roosevelt. An ambitious northern politician, Roosevelt had advanced his career by cozying up to the white southerners who dominated his party. During World War I, while serving as assistant secretary of the navy, he had supported segregation in the armed

Opposite: Franklin D. Roosevelt won election to the presidency in 1932, promising a "new deal" for struggling Americans.

forces. As governor of New York, he had not taken any actions or made any statements in support of civil rights. The NAACP warned that a vote for the Democrats was a vote to extend segregation. One prominent black Republican went further, predicting that a Roosevelt presidency would "put the Negro again into virtual slavery."

In November 1932 more than two-thirds of all African-American voters cast their ballots for the Republican candidate. The number of registered black voters was small, however, mainly because of discriminatory laws that made it difficult or impossible for African Americans to vote. As a result, the black vote had little impact on the election. When all votes were counted, Franklin Roosevelt had won forty-two of the forty-eight states, sweeping Herbert Hoover out of office.

ALPHABET SOUP

During his presidential campaign, Franklin Roosevelt had promised "a new deal for the American people." That New Deal began to take shape immediately after the new president took office in March 1933. During the first one hundred days of Roosevelt's presidency, Congress passed fifteen major pieces of legislation designed to provide relief to the needy, establish economic reforms, and help the country recover from the Depression.

The New Deal legislation created an "alphabet soup" of new government agencies and programs. The agencies that had the greatest impact on African Americans included the Federal Emergency Relief Administration (FERA), the National Recovery Administration (NRA), the Works Progress Administration (WPA), the Agricultural Adjustment Administration (AAA), the Tennessee Valley Authority (TVA), the Public

Works Administration (PWA), the National Youth Administration (NYA), and the Civilian Conservation Corps (CCC).

Workers gather for a hot meal at a Civilian Conservation Corps camp in New Jersey in June 1933.

None of these agencies specifically targeted the hard-hit African-American community. However, most of the New Deal agencies did offer at least some benefits to blacks along with whites. The NYA created work-study programs and part-time jobs for about 300,000 black boys and girls. The CCC put about a quarter of a million black youths to work on projects in national forests, parks, and other public lands. Hundreds of thousands of African-American men and women worked on WPA projects, which included building or improving roads, airports, schools, parks, and waterways. The WPA also supported the work of African-American writers, artists, actors, and musicians. In addition, PWA funds helped build hospitals, college buildings, playgrounds, and low-cost housing in African-American communities.

New Deal or Raw Deal?

While New Deal programs relieved the suffering of many needy Americans, blacks faced an uphill battle to secure their fair share of benefits. The southern white legislators who dominated Congress refused to equip the federal programs with safeguards against racial discrimination and injustice. The day-to-day administration of the programs was assigned to local white officials and employers. In the South these administrators consistently favored whites in the dispensing of relief, jobs, and other benefits.

In 1933 African Americans made up 50 percent of the population of Mississippi but received only 1.7 percent of the state's Civilian Conservation Corps jobs. That same year government inspectors found that there was not a single black foreman or clerical worker in Tennessee Valley Authority projects across the South. Officials for the Agricultural Adjustment Administration looked the other way when white landowners stole benefit checks intended for black sharecroppers. In many cases, AAA programs actually led to increased hardships for black farm families, as landowners evicted sharecroppers from their farms rather than give them their rightful share of benefits. The National Recovery Administration also bowed to discrimination. NRA codes allowed employers in many industries to pay black workers lower

These Missouri sharecroppers were left homeless in 1939 after their landlords evicted them to avoid sharing government benefit payments.

wages than whites. When the agency required equal wages, most southern white employers simply fired their African-American workers. Black newspapers began calling the NRA the "Negro Run Around" or the "Negro Removal Act."

In 1935 black activist John P. Davis denounced the unmet promises of President Roosevelt's relief and recovery programs. Reviewing the gains and losses delivered by the NRA and other agencies, Davis found a record of "vicious" discrimination. "On every hand," he concluded, "the New Deal has used slogans for the same raw deal."

A SECOND CHANCE

By the mid-1930s, a variety of forces, both within and outside the Roosevelt administration, were coming together to transform the "raw deal" into a better deal for blacks. Outside forces included the growing power of black voters as well as cooperation between black leaders and increasing numbers of white supporters in both the North and South. Inside the White House, First Lady Eleanor Roosevelt shared her passionate commitment to civil rights with the president, members of his cabinet, and congressional leaders. Her actions encouraged many federal officials in charge of New Deal programs to work harder for the welfare of all Americans, regardless of race.

Harold Ickes, director of the Public Works Administration, led the way by setting quotas (minimum numbers) for the hiring of African Americans as both skilled and unskilled laborers on PWA construction projects. W. Frank Persons of the Labor Department insisted that African Americans receive a fair share of Civilian Conservation Corps jobs. Aubrey Williams of the National Youth Administration made certain that black and

"FIRST LADY INDEED!"

Franklin Roosevelt believed in "first things first." The president took a cautious approach toward civil rights issues because he believed that his most important task was ensuring America's economic recovery. If he took a stand against racism, he feared that southern lawmakers would "block every bill I ask Congress to pass to keep America from collapsing. I just can't take that risk."

Eleanor Roosevelt had no such reservations. The First Lady frequently spoke out against racial discrimination and injustice. She infuriated many white southerners by visiting black sharecroppers' homes and inviting black visitors to the White House. She also served as a "go-between," presenting the concerns of African-American leaders to her husband and explaining his views to them. Thanks in large part to her influence, the president gradually began to pay more attention to racial matters. He met with civil rights leaders and appointed African Americans to important advisory roles in the federal government.

During President Roosevelt's second term, Eleanor became even more outspoken in her support of civil rights. She supported antilynching legislation and a movement to abolish the poll tax. She spoke at civil rights conventions and defied the Jim Crow system by sitting, eating, and socializing with blacks in the South. Her actions brought endless condemnation and ridicule from the supporters of white supremacy. To African Americans, meanwhile, Eleanor Roosevelt was a source of inspiration and hope. The Urban League called her "the First Lady indeed!" The head of the National Negro Congress applauded Eleanor for "the inspiration she has given us. . . . Now we know that when we raise our voices for more and better jobs, cheaper and more adequate housing, civil liberties and protection from the lynch mob, we have a staunch ally in the First Lady of the Land."

Eleanor Roosevelt outraged white southerners by treating African Americans, young and old, with courtesy and respect.

white youths employed by the agency received equal wages. The directors of other New Deal agencies, including the Federal Works Agency, the Farm Security Administration, and the U.S. Housing Authority, also worked toward equality in benefits and opportunities.

In May 1935 President Roosevelt issued an executive order requiring the Works Progress Administration to assign jobs to people based on their qualifications, without discrimination "on any grounds whatsoever." Congress followed suit, writing antidiscrimination clauses into more than twenty New Deal laws.

The new legislation did not end discrimination by the federal government or by local officials running federal relief programs. Blacks still found it harder than whites to qualify for relief, and they continued to receive lower benefits and wages. Black schools, hospitals, and other public facilities in the South still received far less than their federally mandated shares of New Deal construction funds. However, the number of African Americans receiving relief and the benefits they earned rose steadily during the "second New Deal." The WPA alone provided wages that ensured the survival of one million black families. Millions of dollars were spent building and repairing black schools and other facilities. Black illiteracy dropped 10 percent in the 1930s as one million African Americans took

A New Deal worker helps build a dam on the French Broad River in Tennessee.

advantage of New Deal education programs.

At long last the federal government was beginning to acknowledge its responsibilities to the "forgotten races." Black Americans remained on the bottom rung of the economic ladder, but their hopes and expectations had begun to rise. "For the first time," a black delegation told President Roosevelt in 1939, "Negro men and women have reason to believe that their government does care."

The "Black Cabinet"

One notable sign of progress in the second New Deal was the emergence of the "Black Cabinet." Earlier presidents had occasionally sought advice from prominent black leaders. However, Franklin Roosevelt was the first president to appoint large numbers of black men and women to federal posts. By mid-1935, about forty-five African Americans were serving as advisers in New Deal agencies and cabinet departments. Among them were college presidents, social workers, a newspaper editor, an attorney, an economist, and a labor leader. The press called this group of highly trained, highly educated people the president's Black Cabinet.

Prominent members of the Black Cabinet included Robert C. Weaver, racial adviser in the Federal Housing Administration; William H. Hastie, assistant solicitor in the Department of the Interior; Robert L. Vann, special assistant to the attorney general; Lawrence A. Oxley, chief of the Division of Negro Labor in the Department of Labor; Edgar Brown, adviser on Negro affairs in the Civilian Conservation Corps; and William J. Trent, racial relations officer in the Federal Works Agency. Outranking them all was Mary McLeod

Bethune. Born to a sharecropping family in South Carolina, Bethune had worked her way through school. She had gone on to found a primary school in Florida, which she built into Bethune-Cookman College. Bethune was the first black woman to head a federal agency, serving as the director of the NYA's Office of Minority Affairs.

Mary McLeod Bethune and the other advisers in President Roosevelt's Black Cabinet used their influence to press for economic and political equality for African Americans. They worked closely with the black press and civil rights leaders, sharing information and developing strategies for government reform. One of their most cherished goals was increasing opportunities for other African Americans in industry and government. In 1933 there were about 50,000 black employees in the federal government. Five years later, the number was 82,000 and climbing. While many of these employees worked at unskilled or semiskilled jobs, the group also included clerks, secretaries, librarians, lawyers, economists, architects, engineers, chemists, and physicists. For the first time, educated black men and women were finding a respected place in their nation's government.

This portrait of educator and presidential adviser Mary McLeod Bethune was painted by the German-born artist Winold Reiss.

Don't Go In! ► STOP!
Strike Today!

Model Blouse Employees are ON STRIKE to end firing of UNION members, for JUST hours, FAIR wages, and DECENT working conditions!

★★★

ALL OUT ON THE PICKET LINE FOR A COMPLETE
UNION VICTORY

Amalgamated Clothing Workers of America
19 E. Pine Street, Millville, N. J.

license no. 24

Chapter 3

ORGANIZING FOR ACTION

THE CONGRESSIONAL ELECTIONS OF 1934 marked a turning point in American political history. For the first time, a majority of black voters cast their ballots for Democratic candidates. Two years later, in the 1936 presidential election, both the Republicans and Democrats actively campaigned for the black vote. Republican candidate Alf Landon spoke out against lynching and other attempts "to persecute any minority on grounds of race, religion, or class." Franklin Roosevelt countered by pointing to the millions of African Americans benefiting from his New Deal programs. At massive Democratic rallies, Eleanor Roosevelt joined civil rights leaders in praising Roosevelt as a "second Emancipator." The First Lady also worked with the Good Neighbor League, a political group formed to attract black Republicans to the Democratic side. In its campaign literature, the league urged African Americans to "stop voting for Lincoln and vote for Roosevelt instead."

Opposite: This old poster is evidence of the growing activism of labor unions—including interracial and all-black unions—during the 1930s.

All these efforts paid off. In November 1936 an overwhelming 76 percent of northern blacks voted to reelect Franklin Roosevelt. The Republicans had learned that they could no longer take the black vote for granted. The Democrats had learned the value of a progressive policy toward civil rights. Most importantly, northern blacks had discovered their own political might.

Even in the South, blacks were beginning to make some progress on the political front. The poll tax and other Jim Crow measures still barred most southern blacks from voting. However, the emergence of black political organizations and voter registration drives was beginning to worry many southern whites. A sheriff in Alabama complained that blacks were getting the idea "that they can become regular voters. I think it's dangerous." In Georgia an elections official grumbled over the increase in black voting "since Roosevelt became Santa Claus."

The rise in political activity in both the North and South was a sign of the increasing assertiveness of the struggle for civil rights. While the New Deal was easing some of the hardships of the Great Depression, blacks had come to realize that they could no longer wait and hope for government to meet their needs. Instead, they would have to work together more effectively than ever in the battle for civil rights. Black Americans would not "place their problems for solution down at the feet of their white sympathetic allies," declared black labor leader A. Philip Randolph, "for, in the final analysis, the salvation of the Negro . . . must come from within."

BLACKS IN THE LABOR MOVEMENT

At the start of the Great Depression, most labor unions had a long history of commitment to Jim Crow. Some unions confined black workers to segregated divisions under the authority of local white chapters. Others barred African Americans completely.

African Americans responded by forming their own independent unions. The largest of the all-black unions was the Brotherhood of Sleeping Car Porters and Maids (BSCP), organized by A. Philip Randolph in 1925. Randolph's union represented tens of thousands of porters and maids who worked for the Pullman Company, operator of the nation's railroads.* However, the nation's largest labor alliance, the American Federation of Labor (AFL), refused to recognize the BSCP or any other black union.

A. Philip Randolph believed that the key to African-American advancement was achieving equal rights and opportunities in the workplace.

The first break in the union color bar came in the early 1930s, when the American Communist and Socialist parties began to organize workers in the South. The Communists formed labor alliances including the National Textile Workers and the Sharecropper Union. Their unions welcomed both black and white members. So did the Southern Tenant Farmers Union (STFU), a Socialist union representing sharecroppers and farm laborers. The STFU campaigned not only for economic justice for all its members but also for racial justice for African Americans. While the interracial unions won praise from many black leaders as well as liberal publications such as the *New York Times*, they remained relatively small and powerless.

*For more on A. Philip Randolph and the Brotherhood of Sleeping Car Porters and Maids, see volume 7 in this series, *The Harlem Renaissance.*

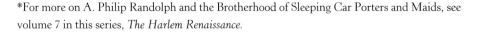

BLACKS AND "REDS"

The suffering and social upheaval of the Great Depression drove some Americans toward radical political movements such as Communism. The American branch of the Communist Party had been established in 1919. By 1938, it had attracted about 75,000 members with its call for radical social change and its support for the rights of oppressed workers. The Communists condemned racism

Children take the lead in a 1933 Communist Party rally in Philadelphia.

and segregation. They helped organize radical civil rights groups, including the American Negro Labor Congress. They also took the lead in defending the Scottsboro Boys, organizing conferences, marches, and rallies to demand freedom for the nine black youths. "I don't care whether they are Reds, Greens, or Blues," said the mother of one of the boys. "They are the only ones who put up a fight to save these boys and I am with them to the end."

Despite the Communists' support for civil rights, only a small proportion of African Americans ever joined the party. Like the great majority of white Americans, most blacks considered the "Reds" unpatriotic and un-American. African Americans were also suspicious of Communist leaders, who often used the race issue as a tool to advance their own purposes. In the early 1940s, both black and white membership in the American Communist Party rapidly declined. The party had never become a major political force in the United States. However, it had made important contributions to the cause of civil rights by publicizing the evils of racism, encouraging interracial cooperation, and inspiring many African Americans to more militant action.

In the early years of the Depression, labor unions faced significant challenges. With unemployment soaring, management held all the cards. If workers were dissatisfied with their wages or working conditions, company owners could always find others willing to fill their jobs. In the early 1930s, AFL membership shrank to about three million, half its pre-Depression size. Meanwhile, one study of black workers mourned "the virtual collapse" of the Brotherhood of Sleeping Car Porters and "Negro labor as a whole."

FROM ENEMY TO ALLY

In 1933 a New Deal law breathed new life into the organized labor movement. Section 7a of the National Industrial Recovery Act encouraged unionizing by giving employees "the right to organize and bargain collectively [as a group] through representatives of their own choosing [without] interference, restraint, or coercion." A new government agency, the National Labor Relations Board, was established to protect workers' rights and settle disputes between employers and employees.

Armed with their New Deal protections, union organizers fanned out across the country, recruiting hundreds of thousands of members for unions both old and new. AFL membership soared. So did the number of organized workers in a new labor alliance, the Committee for Industrial Organization (CIO).

The CIO had been born out of a dispute within the labor movement. The AFL organized workers according to their craft or skilled trade, such as carpentry or typesetting. That meant that employees in the same industry were often organized into several different unions, while many less-skilled workers had no representation at all. John L. Lewis, president of the United

John L. Lewis was a powerful speaker and organizer who fought for the rights of American workers, black and white.

Mine Workers, believed that unions would be stronger if all the workers in a particular industry joined together, regardless of their differences in skill. In 1935 Lewis broke with the AFL and formed the CIO. His new alliance organized the millions of unskilled and semiskilled workers in mass production industries such as auto making and meatpacking.

From the beginning Lewis made it clear that the CIO would organize black workers on an equal basis with whites. Hundreds of thousands of African Americans joined CIO unions including the Steel Workers Organizing Committee, the United Automobile Workers, and the International Ladies' Garment Workers Union. Side by side with white coworkers, black men and women joined in strikes and picket lines to force employers to meet their demands. Union membership brought African-American workers higher wages, better working conditions, and greater job security.

The CIO unions were not completely color-blind. Some unions maintained segregated white and black branches in the

A policeman collars a black laborer during a 1938 garbage collectors' strike in Philadelphia.

South. Even integrated unions often held separate meetings and provided separate facilities for white and black members. Black coal miner Leon Alexander recalled that local laws in Birmingham, Alabama, required segregation during union meetings in the early 1930s.

> We had to go in the back door, and the whites came in the front door. . . . We rebelled against it by just defying the ordinance and walking on in the front door. . . . Then they said we had to sit on separate sides of the hall. We couldn't all sit on the same side, the white had to be on one side and the colored [on the other]. It is laughable!

Despite the lingering discrimination, the organized labor movement became one of the most powerful allies in the struggle for civil rights. The national leaders of CIO unions spoke out against racism and supported legislation to outlaw lynching and abolish the poll tax. Union newspapers and workers' education programs publicized civil rights issues, reaching millions of white Americans who had never thought about questions of discrimination and racial injustice. Even the AFL, faced with competition from the CIO, eventually began to ease restrictions on black membership. In 1935 the Brotherhood of Sleeping Car Porters became the first black union ever granted a charter in the AFL.

The labor movement also advanced the cause of civil rights by giving thousands of black workers their first experiences in voting, negotiating, holding office, and other political skills. Union and nonunion members alike were inspired by the sight of blacks and whites working side by side at all levels of union management. For the first time, many African Americans felt a sense of being part of the larger American society. They were also beginning to recognize the power that is unleashed when people unite and work together for a common goal.

CIVIL RIGHTS GROUPS BATTLE JIM CROW

Labor was just one of the many areas in which African Americans battled for greater rights during the Depression. A variety of civil rights groups also confronted segregation and injustice in other aspects of American life, including education, housing, and voting rights.

The NAACP, the nation's oldest and largest civil rights organization, chose the courts for its main battleground. Among the many talented lawyers working for the NAACP were Harvard graduates William H. Hastie and Charles H. Houston and future Supreme Court justice Thurgood Marshall. In the 1930s these attorneys pursued a number of impor-

tant legal cases aimed at ending segregation, outlawing
lynching, and abolishing the
poll tax and other barriers to
black voting.

Their most celebrated victory involved Jim Crow in
education. A black college
graduate named Lloyd Gaines
had been denied admission to
the University of Missouri law
school because the school did
not accept blacks. Charles H.
Houston took the case all the way to the Supreme Court. In
1938 the Court ruled that the university's segregationist policies violated the Fourteenth Amendment to the Constitution,
which guaranteed all Americans the right to "equal protection
under the laws." Southern states would either have to build
separate and fully equal law schools for black students or admit
blacks to their all-white schools. *Time* magazine reported that
the ruling meant

Attorneys Thurgood
Marshall *(left)* and
Charles Houston *(right)*
represent Donald G.
Murray *(center)*, who
was denied entry to
the University of Mary-
land law school in 1934
because of his race.
Murray won his case in
state court.

far more than a chance [for African Americans] to
go to professional school. The South today spends
only one-fourth as much for each Negro child's
education as for each white child's, and . . . the
court's ruling that Negroes must have equal educational opportunities means that the South must
establish parity [equality] in expenditures from
top to bottom of its school system.

The strongest bond of human sympathy, outside the family relation, should be one uniting all working people

Tenants protest the eviction of a black family from a New York City apartment building in the late 1930s. They were part of the East Side Tenants Union, an organization dedicated to fighting Jim Crow.

While the NAACP battled in the courts, other civil rights groups challenged Jim Crow with tactics ranging from protest marches and rallies to educational campaigns and political action. The Urban League pressured schools, businesses, and government to expand job training and job opportunities for blacks. The Commission on Interracial Cooperation worked to improve understanding and cooperation between the races. African-American women in cities across the nation formed Housewives' Leagues to promote economic self-reliance. The leagues encouraged members to shop at black-owned businesses, buy from black manufacturers, and patronize black professionals.

In 1935 the National Negro Congress (NNC) was established to coordinate the efforts of the hundreds of different civil rights organizations. The challenges of fighting for equality were too great for any one organization, proclaimed the NNC's first president, A. Philip Randolph. African Americans of different classes, occupations, and philosophies would have to unite in order to "rally power and mass support behind vital issues affecting the life and destiny of the race."

"Don't Buy Where You Can't Work"

One of the most effective "mass action" tools against Jim Crow was the boycott. During the 1930s, civil rights groups in

Chicago, Detroit, Boston, Washington, D.C., and dozens of other cities organized boycotts of white-owned businesses that operated in black neighborhoods but refused to hire black workers. Some of the most successful campaigns took place in New York City's Harlem. In 1933 hundreds of African Americans joined the picket lines outside one of Harlem's white-owned department stores, carrying signs that read DON'T BUY WHERE YOU CAN'T WORK. After nearly two months, the store gave in and hired its first black clerks and cashiers.

Adam Clayton Powell Jr. (center) celebrates his victory in the 1958 Democratic congressional primary. Powell went on to win election to his seventh term in the House of Representatives.

Five years later, the Reverend Adam Clayton Powell Jr. led black Harlemites in a community-wide boycott of stores, public utilities, insurance companies, and banks. "Three hundred and fifty thousand consumers are not anything to sneeze at," said the dynamic minister, "and if anyone dares to sneeze, we are killing him with the worst cold he ever had." The boycott resulted in hundreds of jobs for blacks, as well as an agreement that Harlem's white store owners would hire black workers for one-third of all new executive, clerical, and sales jobs. It also launched a political career that would take Adam Clayton Powell all the way to the U.S. House of Representatives, where his uncompromising stand against racism would earn him the nickname Mr. Civil Rights.

African Americans find comfort and fellowship at church, in a painting by Jacob Lawrence.

Chapter 4

AT HOME AND AT PLAY

BEHIND THE WORK OF ALL THE DIFFERENT CIVIL rights organizations was a single goal: breaking down the barriers that prohibited full participation by African Americans in the political, social, and economic life of the nation. Ever since the days of slavery, black Americans had lived largely in their own separate world, apart from whites. The Jim Crow system enforced the separation of the races. The laws of the South required segregation in housing, education, transportation, and most other areas of life. Even in the North, where segregation was not as strictly enforced as in the South, most African Americans lived in crowded city ghettos, where they formed a separate black society within the larger American community.

During the Great Depression, African Americans often looked within the black community for help, strength, and comfort. The members of large extended families shared what little they had. Black mutual aid societies, women's clubs, and churches distributed food, clothing, and emergency shelter and health care. "People who would now be considered below the poverty level," recalled one black woman from North Carolina, "had enough sense of self, of human worth, to enjoy sharing what they had with others."

THE BLACK CHURCH

The black church had always been one of the pillars of African-American society. During the Depression more than ever before, African Americans turned to their churches for both spiritual comfort and more practical assistance. Thousands of Baptist and Methodist churches operated soup kitchens and shelters in cities throughout the nation. In the first three months of 1931 alone, the Abyssinian Baptist Church in Harlem provided needy blacks with 28,500 free meals, nearly 18,000 items of clothing, and more than 2,500 pairs of shoes.

Prayer services at the Abyssinian Baptist Church in Harlem, 1944

Along with the established black churches, the Depression saw an explosion of "storefront churches" in northern cities. These humble establishments were housed in abandoned stores and the basements, attics, and back rooms of homes and apartments. The preachers were self-appointed and self-trained. The worshippers included the poorest and least educated members of the community. Many were downtrodden migrants seeking a spontaneous and emotional form of worship not found in the more traditional churches.

The typical storefront church might have no more than fifty worshippers. Meanwhile, the membership of another type of "homegrown" religious establishment, the evangelical church, often numbered in the tens of thousands. Evangelical churches stressed the literal truth of the Bible and the importance of a personal relationship with God through Jesus Christ. Successful black evangelical leaders included George W. Becton of the World's Gospel Feast in Harlem, Charles Emmanuel "Sweet Daddy" Grace of the United House of Prayer in Washington, D.C., and, most famous of them all, George Baker, known as Father Divine.

Father Divine was born in Maryland in 1879. He spent his early years traveling across the South as an evangelical preacher. In 1919 he moved to Long Island, New York, where he began to attract a following. In his sermons the mesmerizing preacher proclaimed that he had come "to comfort you, bless you, give you homes for your bodies, rest for your souls, relief from all sorrow." His message offered hope and comfort in a time of great suffering. By the mid-1930s, Father Divine's Peace Mission movement included branches, or "kingdoms," stretching from coast to coast. While the movement was interracial, the vast majority of members were black.

Father Divine was more than a spiritual leader. His movement was also a social institution. The Peace Mission kingdoms ran restaurants where needy people could enjoy nourishing ten- or fifteen-cent meals as well as lodging houses where they could rent a room for one dollar a week. The movement also owned and operated grocery stores, barbershops, dry cleaners, and other

Followers of Father Divine's Peace Mission parade through the streets of Harlem in 1938.

businesses that provided jobs for countless followers. In addition, Father Divine investigated and protested cases of racial discrimination, segregation, and lynching. His efforts to feed, clothe, house, and protect the poor led his followers to declare that the minister was God in the flesh. Although Father Divine himself never made such a claim, he never denied it either.

The leaders of traditional black churches denounced Father Divine as a fraud and con man. Some historians have dismissed him as a cult leader. Others consider him an early leader in the civil rights movement, who fought poverty and racism with an imaginative blend of religion, social service, and business smarts.

WRITERS AND ARTISTS

While religion can offer comfort in times of need, people often turn to another source to forget their troubles completely: the

THE NATION OF ISLAM

The religion of Islam traveled to America in the 1600s, with the first black Muslim slaves from Africa. Over time the majority of African Americans adopted Christianity. Then, in 1930, a Detroit preacher named W. D. Fard began a new religious movement based on Islam. Condemning the white race and Christianity, Fard urged African Americans to "reclaim their original identity as Muslims." He taught the followers of his Nation of Islam movement to turn their backs on America's corrupt society and live disciplined, righteous lives "according to the law of Allah." Fard's captivating personality and his message of racial pride attracted thousands of followers.

In 1934 W. D. Fard vanished without a trace. His chief minister, Elijah Poole, carried on his teachings. Changing his name to Elijah Muhammad, the new Nation of Islam leader proclaimed that Fard had been Allah in the flesh and that he, Muhammad, was the Prophet of Allah. Under the leadership of Elijah Muhammad, the Nation of Islam, also known as the Black Muslims, became not only a religion but also a political and social movement. Its many followers denounced racism and rejected the possibility of an interracial solution to America's race problem. Forming a separate sect within American society, they emphasized black self-respect and self-reliance. The Nation of Islam established temples and schools as well as farms, bakeries, restaurants, supermarkets, and apartment houses. During the civil rights movement of the 1950s and 1960s, the often controversial Nation of Islam would achieve national prominence through spokespersons including Malcolm X and boxing champion Muhammad Ali.

Above: Elijah Muhammad led the Nation of Islam during its period of greatest growth, from the mid-1930s through the civil rights movement.

world of entertainment. During the Great Depression, Americans of all races enjoyed an abundant outpouring of literature, art, music, theater, and movies. Black artists and performers not only contributed their share of the entertainment but also led the way in overcoming negative stereotypes of African Americans and presenting a prouder, more accurate image.

Many of the African-American writers, poets, and artists who had soared to fame during the Harlem Renaissance continued to fly high during the Depression.* In addition, a younger generation of writers explored the black experience in America. One of the most notable young writers of the period was Richard Wright. In 1938 Wright published *Uncle Tom's Children*, a collection of four short novels depicting the plight of blacks in the rural South. Two years later, *Native Son* rocketed him to international fame. The best-selling novel told the story of a young black migrant confronted with racism, injustice, and violence in a Chicago ghetto. Wright once said that he had only one goal in writing *Native Son*: "to tell the truth as I saw it and felt it."

The Works Progress Administration (WPA) played an important role in supporting the work of many struggling black writers and artists during the Depression. Jacob Lawrence attended WPA art classes in Harlem as a boy. He completed his education working on WPA art projects. In the late 1930s, he began to demonstrate his talents in wonderful paintings

Jacob Lawrence gained widespread recognition as an artist while serving in the Coast Guard during World War II. The painting in the background is shown in color on the opposite page.

*To learn more about the black writers, artists, and performers of the 1920s and early 1930s, see volume 7 in this series, *The Harlem Renaissance.*

Ironers by Jacob Lawrence, 1943. Art critics have praised Lawrence as a master at using lines, poses, and colors to convey his subjects' moods.

inspired by African-American history. Some of Lawrence's best-known works feature scenes from the lives of abolitionist leaders, including John Brown, Frederick Douglass, and Harriet Tubman. His Great Migration series consists of sixty panels illustrating the journey of African Americans from the rural South to northern cities during the Great Migration. Lawrence had spent much of his childhood journeying up the East Coast with his family. He described his work on the Great Migration series as an intensely personal experience. "It was such a part of me," he said, "that I didn't think of something outside. It was like I was doing a portrait of something. If it was a portrait, it was a portrait of myself, a portrait of my family, a portrait of my peers."

From Swing to the Big Screen

The black musicians of the Harlem Renaissance gave the world jazz, ragtime, and the blues. In the 1930s and 1940s, Renaissance musicians—including blues singer Billie Holiday, jazz trumpeter Louis Armstrong, and bandleaders Duke Ellington, William "Count" Basie, and Cab Calloway—reached new heights of pop-

Hattie McDaniel *(right)* with Vivien Leigh in the 1939 blockbuster film *Gone with the Wind*

ularity. Black musicians also created new forms of music. The jazz "big bands" that had entertained millions during the Renaissance played a hot new sound called swing. Pianist Thelonious Monk, saxophonist Charlie "Yardbird" Parker, trumpeters "Dizzy" Gillespie and Miles Davis, and other black jazzmen experimented with bebop, or bop. This new form of jazz combined complex rhythms, steady beats, and imaginative harmonies.

One of the hottest new musical stars of the 1940s was Lena Horne. Horne's sultry singing voice and glamorous looks made her the first black female superstar. During her long career, she would sing, dance, and perform in Broadway shows and movies. Black women who were used to seeing themselves portrayed on stage and screen as maids and "mammies" took pride in the popular singer-actress who crossed the color line to appear in "mainstream" leading roles.

Other black stars of the stage and screen included Louise Beavers, classical singer Paul Robeson, and tap dancer Bill "Bojangles" Robinson. In 1939 actress Hattie McDaniel became the first African American to win an Academy Award, for her supporting role in *Gone with the Wind*. Some black leaders criticized McDaniel for promoting racial stereotypes by playing the role of a slave "mammy." The actress responded that black actors had little choice in the types of roles they played. "It's much better to play a maid than to be one," said McDaniel. "The only choice permitted me is either to be a servant for $7.00 a week or portray one for $700.00 a week."

"ONCE IN A HUNDRED YEARS"

While Lena Horne and other African-American performers blazed new trails in popular music, black classical performers were also winning acclaim in America and abroad. Opera singer Marian Anderson made her first European tour in the early 1930s. Her concerts received rave reviews. After hearing Anderson perform, the famous Italian conductor Arturo Toscanini exclaimed that a voice like hers was heard "once in a hundred years."

When Marian Anderson returned to the United States, she met with racism and segregation in restaurants, hotels, and concert halls. In 1939 she tried to book an appearance in Washington, D.C.'s Constitution Hall. The renowned singer was rejected. The hall, owned by the Daughters of the American Revolution (DAR), was reserved for white artists only.

Many prominent Americans, both black and white, protested the DAR's racist policies. First Lady Eleanor Roosevelt resigned from the organization over the incident. In the end officials in the Roosevelt administration arranged for Marian Anderson to give a free public concert at the Lincoln Memorial. On Easter Sunday 1939, a mixed-race audience of nearly 75,000 fans gathered to hear the internationally acclaimed star sing a selection of classical music and old-time black spirituals. Concert performer Todd Duncan never forgot the thrill of being part of the audience. "My feelings were so deep," said Duncan.

> I had never been so proud to be an American; I had never been so proud to be an American Negro. . . . The highlight of that day was when this thing [the Lincoln Memorial] became a great citadel, a cathedral. The highlight was the first words that she sang: "My country 'tis of thee, sweet land of liberty, of thee I sing."

Above: Marian Anderson gives a return performance at the Lincoln Memorial in 1952.

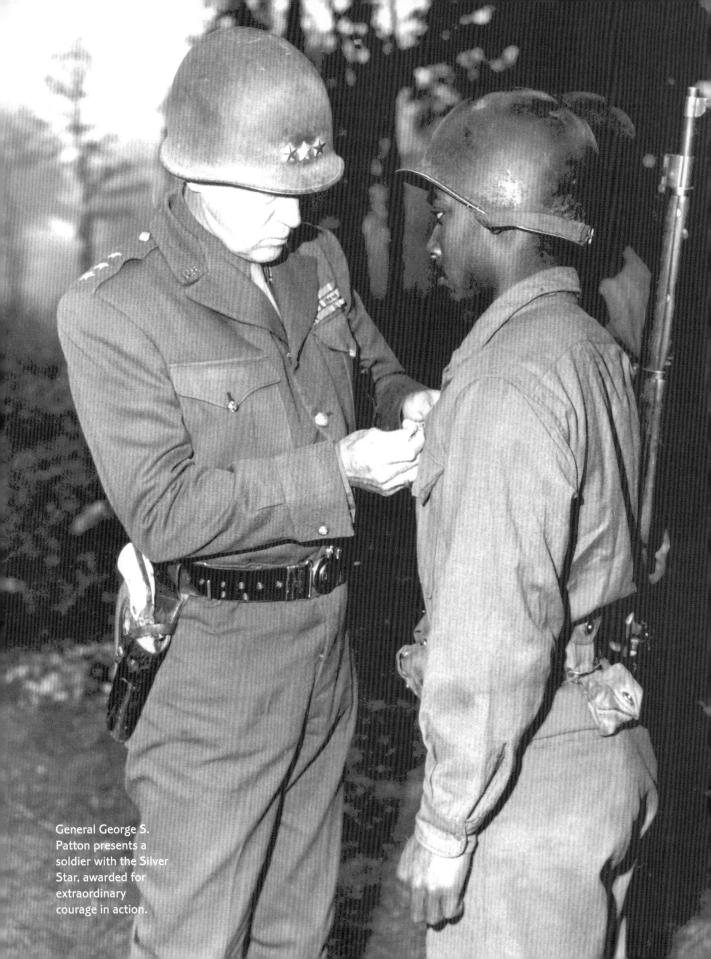

General George S. Patton presents a soldier with the Silver Star, awarded for extraordinary courage in action.

Chapter 5

A Two-Front War

AS AMERICANS STRUGGLED THROUGH THE
Great Depression, war clouds were building in Europe. Adolf
Hitler and his Nazi Party dominated Germany. Benito Mussolini and his Fascists had seized the government of Italy. In
1935 Mussolini invaded the African nation of Ethiopia. Hitler
overran Austria in 1938 and Czechoslovakia in early 1939.
Then, in September 1939, Nazi Germany invaded Poland.
Great Britain and France, which had signed defense agreements with Poland, declared war on Germany. World War II
had begun.

Since the end of World War I, the United States had steered
clear of European politics and conflicts. Most Americans
hoped to stay out of the new conflict. However, they supported
President Roosevelt's pledge to use "all methods short of war"
to defend the nation and help defeat Hitler.

In 1940 Germany continued its ruthless advance across
Europe, swallowing up Norway, Denmark, France, and other

nations. American industry geared up to help Great Britain in its lonely fight for survival. The United States would become the "great arsenal of democracy," providing the British with ships, planes, tanks, guns, ammunition, and other military supplies.

African Americans watched all these developments with mixed emotions. Most had condemned Italy's invasion of Ethiopia and Hitler's rapid rise to power. As one black American saw it, "any individual who becomes a world menace on a doctrine of racial prejudice, bigotry, and oppression . . . is our concern." At the same time, many African Americans asked why they should support a fight for democracy and freedom abroad when they were denied those very rights at home. "Our war is not against Hitler in Europe," proclaimed one black columnist, "but against the Hitlers in America."

THE MARCH ON WASHINGTON

America's rapid defense buildup put an end to the Great Depression. As factories began to crank out military supplies, the demand for both skilled and unskilled workers reached an all-time high. As always, blacks were denied their fair share of opportunities. Most of the new defense jobs were open to whites only. When African Americans did find work, they were usually restricted to low-paying unskilled jobs. In addition, government-sponsored defense training programs discriminated against African Americans. One federal program designed to train workers for skilled manufacturing jobs provided nearly twice as much funding for whites as for blacks.

When black leaders protested the inequalities, federal officials issued statements opposing discrimination in defense jobs. Their halfhearted measures brought few results, however.

RACISM TAKES A BEATING

The 1936 Summer Olympics were held in Berlin, Germany. For Adolf Hitler, it was the perfect opportunity to prove his theory of "Aryan" superiority. The German dictator was confident that his blond-haired, blue-eyed Aryan athletes would easily defeat their "racially inferior" black rivals. Instead, Hitler watched in dismay as African-American track star Jesse Owens broke eleven Olympic records, winning four gold medals.

Two years later, Joe Louis dealt another blow to Nazi racism. The African-American boxer had lost an earlier bout with German boxing champion Max Schmeling. Following that defeat, Louis had gone on to become the world heavyweight boxing champion. In 1938 he faced Schmeling again. This time the black boxer knocked out his white opponent in the first round. That victory made him one of the most popular athletes of any American, black or white. Singer Lena Horne summed up what the Brown Bomber meant to African Americans: "Joe was the one invincible Negro, the one who stood up to the white man and beat him down with his fists."

Above: Harlem residents listen to a radio broadcast of Joe Louis's stunning victory over Max Schmeling in 1938.

Finally, black labor leader A. Philip Randolph concluded that government leaders would "never give the Negro justice until they see masses . . . on the White House lawn."

In early 1941 Randolph warned President Roosevelt that African Americans would descend on the nation's capital in a peaceful protest march unless the federal government protected their rights. The March on Washington was planned for July 1. Black civil rights groups, churches, and other organizations across the nation rallied African Americans to the cause. As support grew, government leaders became alarmed. A massive protest in the nation's capital would embarrass the president, and conflicts between the protesters and white Washingtonians could lead to violence. On June 18 Roosevelt called Randolph and NAACP president Walter White to the White House. The president tried to persuade the two leaders to cancel the march. When that failed, he asked, "Walter, how many people will really march?"

"No less than one hundred thousand," replied White.

Roosevelt looked the black leader straight in the eye. "What do you want me to do?"

One week later, President Roosevelt issued Executive Order 8802. The order banned racial discrimination in government, defense industries, and training programs. The president also established the Fair Employment Practices Committee (FEPC) to investigate cases of discrimination.

Proclaiming victory, black leaders called off the March on Washington. They had not achieved all their objectives. Roosevelt's executive order did not address discrimination in labor unions or the armed services. It did not give the FEPC the authority to force defiant white employers to end their discrim-

At the beginning of World War II, black men who joined the navy could serve only as "messmen," or kitchen attendants.

inatory hiring practices. However, the order marked the first time the federal government had ever taken an official stand against discrimination in employment. It showed what African Americans could accomplish through nonviolent mass action. The successful outcome of the protest would inspire black leaders to intensify their demands for full equality.

On December 7, 1941, the Japanese attacked Pearl Harbor, propelling the United States into World War II. One day later, the NAACP gave notice that African Americans would not put aside their battle for civil rights in support of the war effort. Instead, they would wage a two-front battle, fighting for democracy both at home and abroad. "We shall not abate one iota [bit] our struggle for full citizenship rights here in the United States," NAACP leaders declared. "We will fight, but we demand the right to fight as equals."

JIM CROW AT WAR

Before 1940, African Americans could not enlist in the marines or air force. Black men who joined the army or navy served in all-black units, where they worked mainly as laborers, kitchen and laundry attendants, and officers' servants. Then Congress passed the Selective Service Act of 1940, banning discrimination in the drafting and training of men for military service. All men, regardless of race, could now join any branch of the armed services.

Despite the new law, discrimination persisted. Some local draft boards continued to accept white men only. Blacks who were drafted or who volunteered for service were still assigned to segregated units. Black officers were not permitted to command white troops. Even in the segregated black units, all the top commanders were white. To one African-American officer, it seemed that white commanders "would sit up nights trying to think of ways to keep the Negro soldier, particularly the officers, in 'their place.'"

The War Department responded to protests against the discrimination by establishing a "quota system." Black men would be admitted into the army in numbers based on the percentage of African Americans in the total U.S. population. In addition, a few African Americans were appointed or promoted to higher positions in the military. Colonel Benjamin O. Davis became the first black brigadier general. William H. Hastie was named civilian aide to the secretary of war, and Colonel Campbell C. Johnson became executive assistant to the director of the Selective Service. These small gestures did little to banish Jim Crow from the armed forces, however. For most of World War II, the United States would wage the battle for freedom and democracy overseas with two armies, one black and one white.

BLACK HEROES OF WORLD WAR II

In spite of the discrimination in the armed services, about one million black men and women served their country during

World War II. The vast majority joined the army. Black men also served in the navy, marines, merchant marines, coast guard, and air force. In addition, about four thousand black women volunteered as military nurses or joined the WACs (Women's Army Corps) or the navy's WAVES (Women Accepted for Volunteer Emergency Service).

Racism did not end when black servicemen and women put on their uniforms. In the army African Americans were assigned mainly to service and support roles. While white soldiers finished their training and headed overseas, frustrated black soldiers remained behind. "We were ready to go," remembered infantryman Dennett Harrod. "And we were sick and tired of playing games. We kept getting more badges and citations for good training, but they would just send us back to do some more training."

Finally, in early 1944, the army sent two black divisions to war. The Ninety-third Infantry Division fought the Japanese in the South Pacific islands. The Ninety-second Infantry Division, known as the Buffalo Soldiers, battled German forces in Italy. Both of the segregated units proved themselves under fire, earning hundreds of military decorations for outstanding service and courage.

African Americans in other branches of the armed forces also proved themselves in combat. Black marines played a major

Black soldiers man an antiaircraft battery near the front lines in Italy, 1944.

DORIE MILLER
*Received the Navy Cross
at Pearl Harbor, May 27, 1942*

The navy featured the heroic seaman Dorie Miller in a World War II recruiting poster.

role in key battles in the Pacific region. Black seamen won praise from navy officials for their skill and daring. The most famous black seaman—and the first hero of World War II—was Dorie Miller. Miller was serving as a messman (kitchen attendant) aboard the battleship *West Virginia* when the Japanese attacked Pearl Harbor. Leaping to an unmanned machine gun, the courageous cook began blazing away. He shot down at least four enemy planes before running out of ammunition. Miller was awarded the Navy Cross for his extraordinary bravery and devotion to duty.

Some of the most celebrated black heroes of World War II belonged to the air force. Black air force cadets trained at a segregated facility built at Tuskegee University in Alabama. About five hundred "Tuskegee Airmen" served overseas, battling German fighter planes in the skies over North Africa, Sicily, and Italy. They were credited with destroying 261 German planes and sinking one enemy destroyer. Their successes helped banish any lingering doubts that black servicemen were as capable and courageous as whites. "We were focused on the task," recalled combat pilot Lemuel Curtis, "didn't feel like pioneers or anything. Later, looking back, we realized our trailblazing role."

ON THE HOME FRONT

As American forces fought overseas, violence also plagued the home front. During World War II, large numbers of African Americans migrated to the North and West seeking work at

A white mob wielding sticks and bottles pursues a black man during the 1943 Detroit race riots.

defense plants and shipyards. Fierce competition for jobs and housing in overcrowded cities led to frequent clashes between the races.

In the summer of 1943, race riots broke out in cities including Springfield, Massachusetts; Los Angeles, California; El Paso and Port Arthur, Texas; and New York City's Harlem. The worst violence took place in Detroit, Michigan. Since 1940, nearly a half million people, both black and white, had moved to Detroit. Racial tensions boiled over on the sweltering night of June 20, 1943. A fight between white and black teenagers at a crowded amusement park quickly swelled into a citywide riot. Gangs of young black men roamed the streets, smashing store windows and assaulting white passersby. Meanwhile, white mobs dragged black people out of stores, theaters, and streetcars, beating or shooting them. By the time federal troops restored order two days later, thirty-four people had been killed and hundreds more were injured.

"WHAT ARE WE FIGHTING FOR?"

African-American servicemen stationed in the South faced segregation both within and outside the military. One soldier described a typical encounter with Jim Crow. The anger and humiliation that followed these kinds of incidents led to frequent clashes between southern white civilians and black troops during World War II.

Nine of us, all colored soldiers, were on our way . . . to the hospital at Fort Huachuca, Arizona. After having been crowded like cattle in one coach from Alexandria, Louisiana, we arrived [but] had to wait for our train for about twelve hours. . . . We could not purchase a cup of coffee at any place around the station. The only place that would serve us was the lunchroom at the station. But we couldn't eat where the white people were eating. . . . About two dozen German prisoners of war came into the lunchroom with two guards. They entered the large room, sat at the table. Their meals were served them. They smoked and had a swell time. As we stood on the outside and saw what was going on, we could scarcely believe our own eyes. They were enemies of our country, people sworn to destroy all the so-called democratic governments of the world. . . . What are we fighting for?

Above: An army radioman on the Pacific island of Saipan, 1944

Violent incidents also took place around army training camps. Black recruits trained at camps throughout the United States, including several in the South. Northerners were outraged by the southern Jim Crow laws that banned them from whites-only buses, streetcars, train coaches, shops, theaters, and restaurants. When the soldiers tried to resist the discriminatory treatment, they clashed with the white southerners living near the military bases.

Other racial incidents grew out of the hostility of some white soldiers toward black soldiers who asserted their rights. At Freeman Field, Indiana, more than one hundred black officers were arrested for trying to enter an all-white officers club. At Camp Shenango, Pennsylvania, a fight broke out after a black soldier tried to buy a beer at the whites-only military store. Later, six truckloads of white soldiers retaliated by opening fire on a group of black recruits. "Everybody started scrambling like hell," recalled black army veteran Dempsey Travis. "I was shot three times. . . . Shot not by the enemy but by Americans." Between 1942 and 1945, similar conflicts between soldiers led to full-fledged riots at several military posts, including Fort Dix in New Jersey, Camp Robinson in Arkansas, and Fort Bragg in North Carolina.

On May 7, 1945, Germany surrendered. The surrender of Japan followed on August 14, ending World War II. In spite of the discrimination they faced, African Americans had served their country courageously, helping to bring freedom to millions of people across the world. Now they would return to complete their battle for liberty and justice at home.

IF NEGRO MEN CAN CARRY GUNS FOR UNCLE SAM <u>SURELY</u> THEY CAN DRIVE MILK WAGONS FOR BOWMAN DAIRY

Negro Labor Relation League

Black service overseas inspired increasing protests against unfair labor practices and other forms of racial discrimination at home.

Chapter 6

The Rising Wind

THE WINDS OF CHANGE WERE IN THE AIR AS African Americans came home from service in World War II. Some of the racial barriers in employment and the military had fallen. Inspired by the advances of the war years, black soldiers and civilians alike were no longer willing to put up with a lifetime of injustice. They knew that the promise of racial progress following World War I had led to disappointment. This time, they were determined, things would be different.

The returning soldiers found that there had been little real change in the day-to-day lives of most African Americans. They remained second-class citizens, enduring discrimination in many areas of American government and society. In the North most blacks were still restricted to overcrowded city ghettos. In the South the Jim Crow system still ruled. The laws barring blacks from whites-only housing, schools, restaurants, theaters, and other public places made it impossible for the two races to live on anything close to an equal basis. The postwar years would bring even harsher restrictions, as southern whites struggled to hold on to a way of life based on white supremacy and the suppression of black rights.

"To Secure These Rights"

In July 1946 Roger Malcom, a young black sharecropper in Georgia, got into a fight with his landlord. After stabbing the white man, Roger was thrown in jail. Another white landowner, Loy Harrison, agreed to pay his bail. On July 25 Roger left the jailhouse and joined his wife, Dorothy; Dorothy's brother, George, an army veteran; and George's wife, Mae. Loy Harrison had offered to drive the two black couples home. Instead, the white man drove them to the Moore's Ford Bridge on the Apalachee River, where a lynch mob was waiting. The armed white men dragged the couples from the car and forced them down a path to the river. They stabbed, mutilated, and killed Roger. Then they disposed of the witnesses. As the women screamed for mercy, the lynchers fired again and again, riddling the bodies of Dorothy, Mae, and George with bullets. No one was ever prosecuted for the grisly murders.

The Moore's Ford atrocity was just one of a series of lynchings following World War II. Southern whites were outraged by the newly assertive attitude of southern blacks, especially veterans, and they were determined to reassert white supremacy. In late 1946 an NAACP delegation took a report of the violence to the White House.

The black leaders met with Harry Truman, who had become president after the death of Franklin Roosevelt in April 1945.

Friends and relatives mourn the two young couples murdered by a lynch mob at Moore's Ford Bridge in 1946.

African Americans had mourned Roosevelt's passing. They had worried that the new president might not be as sympathetic to the cause of civil rights. Truman's response to the accounts of racial violence was reassuring. "My God," he exclaimed. "I had no idea it was as terrible as that! We've got to do something!"

President Truman quickly appointed an interracial commission to investigate the status of civil rights in the United States and make recommendations for improvement. The commission issued its final report in October 1947. "To Secure These Rights: The Report of the President's Committee on Civil Rights" documented the widespread abuses of African Americans' rights. It called for a bold program of reform, including federal antilynching legislation, protection of voting rights, and laws guaranteeing equal opportunities in housing, education, and employment.

Southern whites were outraged by the presidential commission's recommendations. They vowed to vote Truman out of office if he tried to carry out the civil rights reforms. Despite their opposition, the president called on Congress to pass the measures proposed by the commission. Truman also issued Executive

Demonstrators carry four empty coffins during a silent march held in San Francisco, California, to protest the Moore's Ford lynchings.

Order 9981, abolishing segregation in the armed forces.

In November 1948 Harry Truman faced one of the most hotly contested presidential races in American history. Strong opposition from white southerners in the newly formed "Dixiecrat" party nearly defeated him. In the end the support of black voters in several northern and western states helped Truman squeak out a narrow victory. But Congress and the American people were becoming increasingly conservative. Over the next four years, Truman would find little support for civil rights reforms. The president would succeed in integrating the military, strengthening the federal civil rights division, and appointing African Americans to high-ranking government positions. Most of the other recommendations of his commission on civil rights, however, would go unanswered.

SIGNS OF PROGRESS

The crucial role played by black voters in the 1948 presidential election was a sign of a major change in America's racial landscape. The steady migration of African Americans from the South meant that black voters now held the balance of power in several cities and states in the North and West. The number of black elected officials was rising at all levels of government, from city councils to state legislatures to the U.S. Congress. These officials used their influence to fight for better opportunities for African Americans in jobs, housing, education, and other areas. An increasing number of blacks were also registering and voting in the South. In 1946 tens of thousands of black Georgians had cast their first ballots in their state's Democratic primary. Over the next few years, the barriers to black voting would begin to weaken in other southern states, including South Carolina and North Carolina.

The postwar years also brought some improvements in employment opportunities. Growing numbers of professionals, teachers, and government employees swelled the black middle class. More African Americans than ever before worked in factories, especially in the thriving aircraft, automobile, electronics, and chemical industries. More labor unions were opened to black workers, giving them powerful allies in their struggle for better jobs and higher wages.

Black organizations, especially the NAACP, played a leading role in the postwar gains against Jim Crow. In 1946 NAACP lawyers won a groundbreaking case challenging segregation in interstate travel. They also challenged the "restrictive covenants" that enforced housing segregation in nearly every American city. Restrictive covenants were agreements written by white property owners that prohibited buyers from reselling or renting their property to blacks. In 1948 the Supreme Court ruled that restrictive covenants could not be enforced in court.

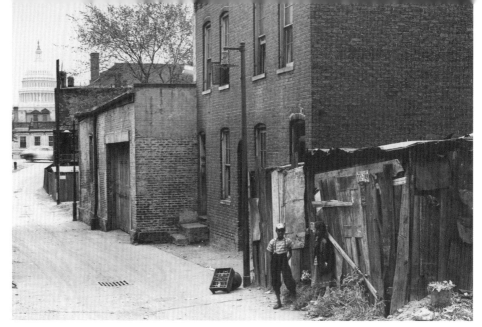

Even in the nation's capital, racial prejudice and discrimination restricted most African Americans to all-black ghettos.

Another significant sign of racial progress was the desegregation of the military. President Truman's Executive Order 9981 met its first test during the Korean War. At the start of that conflict in 1950, most black troops still served in segregated units. By the war's end in 1953, 95 percent of black soldiers had served side by side with whites. The army's officer training school had been opened to all qualified candidates, regardless of race. African-American officers had commanded both white and black troops. General Matthew Ridgway, commander of U.S. troops in Korea, enthusiastically endorsed America's new integrated fighting forces. "Each soldier stands proudly on his own feet," declared Ridgway, "knowing himself to be as good as the next fellow and better than the enemy."

BROWN V. BOARD OF EDUCATION

The postwar advances in civil rights did not come without a price. Racist whites strongly opposed integration in housing, employment, and other areas. African Americans who stood up for their rights often met with threats and violence. One of the most heated battlegrounds between the opponents and sup-

MARCHING TOWARD FREEDOM

BREAKING BASEBALL'S COLOR LINE

In baseball, as in most other sports, black athletes were barred from the whites-only professional teams. The best black ballplayers belonged to the segregated teams of the Negro Baseball Leagues. Branch Rickey, general manager of the Brooklyn Dodgers, disapproved of baseball's color line. In 1945 Rickey offered Jack Roosevelt Robinson a challenge. The twenty-six-year-old shortstop with the Negro League's Kansas City Monarchs was a superb athlete. But was he strong enough to take the abuse and pressure that would come with being the first African American in the major leagues?

Jackie Robinson hits his first home run for the Brooklyn Dodgers.

In April 1947 Jackie Robinson began his first season with the Brooklyn Dodgers. He endured endless ridicule, insults, and threats from white fans, players, and coaches. Through it all, Robinson somehow managed to hold his temper and resist the urge to strike back. Gradually his teammates and even opposing players came to admire and respect him. Meanwhile, his courage and spectacular playing style made him a hero to thousands of fans, black and white.

Jackie Robinson helped lead his team to the 1947 National League pennant. He won the Rookie of the Year award and the 1949 National League's Most Valuable Player award, and eventually entered the National Baseball Hall of Fame. His leadership paved the way for other talented black athletes in professional sports. Years later, Robinson would write that he

> never cared about acceptance as much as I cared about respect. . . . I have always fought for what I believed in. I have had a great deal of support and I have tried to return that support with my best effort. However there is one irrefutable [undeniable] fact of my life which has determined much of what happened to me: I was a black man in a white world.

porters of Jim Crow was the schools.

Ever since the end of Reconstruction, public schools had been strictly segregated in the South. The 1896 Supreme Court ruling in the case of *Plessy* v. *Ferguson* had upheld the "separate but equal" doctrine. Under that policy, states could provide for the separation of the races in public places as long as the facilities were roughly equal.* In practice, segregated facilities for blacks were nearly always inferior to those available to whites. Black schools were run-down, overcrowded, and underfunded. Poorly paid teachers struggled to teach large classes without adequate textbooks, paper, pencils, and other supplies.

The NAACP had spent years fighting for improvements in black education. Lloyd Gaines's suit against the University of Missouri law school (see page 39) and other legal cases had chipped away at the "separate but equal" policy in higher education. Finally, NAACP lawyer Thurgood Marshall decided that it was time to tackle the foundations of Jim Crow. In 1951 Marshall took the case of *Brown* v. *Board of Education* to the Supreme Court. The landmark case combined five separate legal challenges to school segregation, including a suit filed by Oliver Brown of Topeka, Kansas, whose daughter had been denied admission to an all-white elementary school.

Thurgood Marshall argued that school segregation violated the Fourteenth Amendment's guarantee of equal protection under the law. The Supreme Court agreed. On May 17, 1954, Chief Justice Earl Warren read the unanimous decision:

Graduate student George McLaurin sits at a desk outside a classroom at the University of Oklahoma in 1948. Forced by a state court to admit blacks, the university placed him in a segregated corner.

*For more on the *Plessy* v. *Ferguson* case, see volume 6 in this series, *The Rise of Jim Crow.*

We conclude that, in the field of public education, the doctrine of "separate but equal" has no place. Separate educational facilities are inherently [by their nature] unequal. Therefore, we hold that the plaintiffs [the persons bringing the legal action] and others similarly situated . . . are, by reason of the segregation complained of, deprived of the equal protection of the laws guaranteed by the Fourteenth Amendment.

The decision was a monumental triumph in the battle for civil rights. At last the nation's highest court had ruled against segregation. But the battle against Jim Crow was far from over. While some southern districts began to slowly integrate their schools, most vowed to use any means necessary to resist desegregation. Meanwhile, hundreds of thousands of white southerners joined White Citizens Councils and other groups dedicated to maintaining segregation in all areas of public life.

African Americans were equally resolved to see their battle through to a complete and final victory. "A wind *is* rising," wrote NAACP leader Walter White, "a wind of determination by the have-nots of the world to share the benefits of freedom and prosperity which the haves of the earth have tried to keep exclusively for themselves." Over the following decade, that rising wind would build into the hurricane known as the modern civil rights movement.

Two girls meet across the aisle on the first day of desegregation at a Virginia elementary school.

Glossary

Allah the Arabic word for God

Aryan a term used for a prehistoric people of Central Asia, which Adolf Hitler distorted to describe his so-called Master Race of blond, blue-eyed Germans and other northern Europeans

blues a type of music with mournful lyrics that grew out of traditional slave laments and work songs

emancipation freeing someone from the control or power of another

Great Migration a mass migration of African Americans from southern rural areas to northern industrial centers from around 1915 to 1930

Harlem Renaissance an intellectual and cultural flowering in the African-American community that reached its peak in the Harlem section of New York City during the 1920s and early 1930s

Islam the religious faith of Muslims, which is based on the belief that there is only one God and that Muhammad is his prophet, or messenger

Jim Crow laws and practices designed to segregate African Americans, stripping them of their political and civil rights

Muslims followers of Islam

poll tax a discriminatory tax imposed in many southern states following Reconstruction, which was intended to prevent African Americans from voting

ragtime an American music form that reached its height of popularity in the 1910s; ragtime featured "ragged," or syncopated, rhythms

segregation the practice of separating one race from another by setting up separate housing, schools, and other public facilities

sharecropper a tenant farmer who works a plot of land owned by someone else, paying rent by giving the landowner a share of the crops raised

stereotypes exaggerated, usually negative images of people belonging to a particular ethnic group, region, or religion

To Find Out More

BOOKS

Dornfeld, Margaret. *The Turning Tide, 1948–1956: From the Desegregation of the Armed Forces to the Montgomery Bus Boycott.* New York: Chelsea House, 1995.

George, Charles. *Life under the Jim Crow Laws.* San Diego, CA: Lucent Books, 2000.

Hine, Darlene Clark. *The Path to Equality: From the Scottsboro Case to the*

Breaking of Baseball's Color Barrier (1931–1947). New York: Chelsea House, 1995.

Katz, William Loren. *World War II to the New Frontier, 1940–1963*. Austin, TX: Raintree Steck-Vaughn, 1993.

Robinson, Jackie, and Alfred Duckett. *I Never Had It Made*. New York: G. P. Putnam's, 1972.

Trotter, Joe William, Jr. *From a Raw Deal to a New Deal?: African Americans, 1929–1945*. New York: Oxford University Press, 1996.

WEB SITES

African American Odyssey: The Depression, The New Deal, and World War II. Library of Congress.
http://memory.loc.gov/ammem/aaohtml/exhibit/aopart8.html

African-Americans in World War II. The History Place.
http://www.historyplace.com/unitedstates/aframerwar/index.html

Jackie Robinson. TIME for Kids, Time Inc.
http://www.timeforkids.com/TFK/specials/articles/0,6709,714576,00.html

Jazz in Time: The Great Depression. Public Broadcasting Service.
http://www.pbs.org/jazz/time/time_depression.htm

Remembering Jim Crow. American RadioWorks and the Center of Documentary Studies, Duke University.
http://americanradioworks.publicradio.org/features/remembering

The Rise and Fall of Jim Crow. Public Broadcasting Service.
http://www.pbs.org/wnet/jimcrow

Selected Bibliography

Anderson, Jervis. *This Was Harlem, 1900–1950*. New York: Farrar Strauss Giroux, 1982.

Chafe, William H., and others, eds. *Remembering Jim Crow: African Americans Tell About Life in the Segregated South*. New York: New Press, 2001.

Franklin, John Hope, and Alfred A. Moss Jr. *From Slavery to Freedom: A History of African Americans*. New York: Alfred A. Knopf, 2000.

Gates, Henry Louis Jr., and Cornel West. *The African-American Century: How Black Americans Have Shaped Our Country*. New York: Free Press, 2000.

Horton, James Oliver, and Lois E. Horton. *Hard Road to Freedom: The Story of African America*. New Brunswick, NJ: Rutgers University Press, 2001.

Meltzer, Milton. *The Black Americans: A History in Their Own Words, 1619–1983*. New York: HarperTrophy, 1984.

Morehouse, Maggi M. *Fighting in the Jim Crow Army*. Lanham, MD: Rowman and Littlefield, 2000.

Packard, Jerrold M. *American Nightmare: The History of Jim Crow*. New York: St. Martin's Press, 2002.

Rubel, David. *The Coming Free: The Struggle for African-American Equality*. New York: DK Publishing, 2005.

Shapiro, Herbert. *White Violence and Black Response: From Reconstruction to Montgomery*. Amherst, MA: University of Massachusetts Press, 1988.

Sitkoff, Harvard. *A New Deal for Blacks: The Emergence of Civil Rights as a National Issue*. Vol. 1, *The Depression Decade*. New York: Oxford University Press, 1978.

Turner, Richard Brent. *Islam in the African-American Experience*. Bloomington, IN: Indiana University Press, 1997.

Watts, Jill. *God, Harlem U.S.A.: The Father Divine Story*. Berkeley, CA: University of California Press, 1992.

Weinstein, Allen, and Frank Otto Gatell. *The Segregation Era 1863–1954: A Modern Reader*. New York: Oxford University Press, 1970.

Wesley, Charles H. *The Quest for Equality: From Civil War to Civil Rights*. Cornwells Heights, PA: Publishers Agency, 1978.

Notes on Quotes

Chapter 1: The Great Depression

pp. 11–12, "A middle-aged black woman": Meltzer, *The Black Americans*, p. 215.

p. 13, "given up their homes": ibid, p. 213.

p. 14, "a large mass of Negroes": Sitkoff, *A New Deal for Blacks*, p. 39.

p. 14, "Henry Robinson lived": Meltzer, *The Black Americans*, p. 228.

p. 15, "Ain't make nothing": ibid, p. 227.

p. 16, "In March 1931": Trotter, *From a Raw Deal to a New Deal?* p. 51.

p. 17, "a white man's country": Packard, *American Nightmare*, p. 151.

p. 18, "typical lynching is in": Shapiro, *White Violence and Black Response*, p. 219.

p. 18, "No Jobs": Sitkoff, *A New Deal for Blacks*, p. 36.

pp. 18–19, "Mississippi, in": Shapiro, *White Violence and Black Response*, p. 254.

Chapter 2: A New Deal

p. 22, "put the Negro again": Sitkoff, *A New Deal for Blacks*, p. 40.

p. 22, "a new deal": "Roosevelt's Nomination Address, July 2, 1932," at http://www.feri.org/archives/speeches/jul0232.cfm.

p. 25, "Negro Run Around" and "Negro Removal Act": Sitkoff, *A New Deal for Blacks*, p. 55.

p. 25, "On every hand": John P. Davis, "A Black Inventory of the New Deal," *The Crisis*, May 1935, at
http://www.acad.carleton.edu/curricular/hist/classes/Hist121/davis.html.

p. 26, "block every bill": Sitkoff, *A New Deal for Blacks*, p. 46.

p. 26, "the First Lady indeed": ibid, p. 64.

p. 26, "the inspiration she has": ibid, p. 65.

p. 27, "on any grounds whatsoever": ibid, p. 69.

p. 28, "For the first time": ibid, p. 83.

Chapter 3: Organizing for Action

p. 31, "to persecute any minority": Sitkoff, *A New Deal for Blacks*, p. 93.

p. 31, "stop voting for Lincoln": ibid, p. 95.

p. 32, "that they can become": ibid, p. 98.

p. 32, "since Roosevelt became Santa Claus": ibid.

p. 32, "place their problems": Shapiro, *White Violence and Black Response*, p. 257.

p. 34, "I don't care whether": Sitkoff, *A New Deal for Blacks*, p. 147.

p. 35, "the virtual collapse": ibid, p. 175.

p. 35, "the right to organize": "Section 7a, National Industrial Recovery Act" at http://newdeal.feri.org/survey/34213.htm.

p. 37, "We had to go": Chafe and others, *Remembering Jim Crow*, pp. 232–233.

p. 39, "equal protection under the laws": "Fourteenth Amendment to the U.S. Constitution" at http://www.nps.gov/archive/malu/documents/amend14.htm.

p. 39, "far more than a chance": "Damnify Both Races," *Time*, December 26, 1938, at http://www.time.com/time/magazine/
article/0,9171,772192,00.html.

p. 40, "rally power and mass": Shapiro, *White Violence and Black Response*, p. 258.

p. 41, "Don't Buy Where You": Wesley, *The Quest for Equality*, p. 174.

p. 41, "Three hundred and fifty thousand": Horton and Horton, *Hard Road to Freedom*, p. 259.

Chapter 4: At Home and at Play

p. 44, "People who would now": Jacqueline Jones, *Labor of Love, Labor of Sorrow* (New York: Basic Books, 1985), p. 230.

p. 45, "to comfort you": Anderson, *This Was Harlem*, p. 251.

p. 47, "reclaim their original identity": Turner, *Islam in the African-American Experience*, p. 150.

p. 47, "according to the law": ibid, p. 151.

p. 48, "to tell the truth": Gates and West, *The African-American Century*, p. 192.

p. 49, "It was such a part": "The Migration Series" at
http://www.whitney.org/jacoblawrence/art/migration_series.html.

p. 50, "It's much better": Pomerance, *Repeal of the Blues*, p. 89.

p. 51, "once in a hundred years": Gates and West, *The African-American Century*, p. 115.

p. 51, "My feelings were so": "Eleanor Roosevelt and the Marian Anderson Concert" at http://www.exploredc.org/pdfs/marionanderson.pdf.

Chapter 5: A Two-Front War

p. 53, "all methods short of war": Peter Calvocoressi and Guy Wint, *Total War: The Story of World War II* (New York: Random House, 1972), p. 184.

p. 54, "great arsenal of democracy": "Franklin Delano Roosevelt: The Great Arsenal of Democracy" at
http://www.americanrhetoric.com/speeches/fdrarsenalofdemocracy.html.

p. 54, "any individual who becomes": Horton and Horton, *Hard Road to Freedom*, p. 260.

p. 54, "Our war is not": Weinstein and Gatell, *The Segregation Era*, p. 239.

p. 55, "Joe was the one": Horton and Horton, *Hard Road to Freedom*, p. 261.

p. 56, "never give the Negro": Richard Polenberg, *War and Society: The United States, 1941–1945* (New York: J. B. Lippincott, 1972), p. 114.

p. 56, "Walter, how many people": Sitkoff, *A New Deal for Blacks*, p. 320.

p. 57, "We shall not abate": ibid, p. 324.

p. 58, "would sit up nights": Morehouse, *Fighting in the Jim Crow Army*, p. 28.

p. 59, "We were ready": ibid, p. 38.

p. 60, "We were focused on": Jacqueline Harris, *The Tuskegee Airmen: Black Heroes of World War II* (Parsippany, NJ: Dillon Press, 1996), p. 31.

p. 62, "Nine of us, all": Wesley, *The Quest for Equality*, p. 182.

p. 63, "Everybody started scrambling": Studs Terkel, *"The Good War": An Oral History of World War Two* (New York: Pantheon, 1984), pp. 152, 153.

Chapter 6: The Rising Wind

p. 67, "My God": Rubel, *The Coming Free*, p. 41.

p. 70, "Each soldier stands proudly": Wesley, *The Quest for Equality*, p. 196.

p. 71, "never cared about acceptance": Robinson, *I Never Had It Made*, p. 287.

p. 73, "We conclude that": "*Brown* v. *Board of Education*" at
http://www.nationalcenter.org/brown.html.

p. 73, "A wind *is* rising": Allan M. Winkler, *Home Front U.S.A.: America during World War II* (Arlington Heights, IL: Harlan Davidson, 1986), p. 66.

Index

About the Author

VIRGINIA SCHOMP has written more than sixty titles for young readers on topics including dolphins, dinosaurs, occupations, American history, and world history. Ms. Schomp earned a Bachelor of Arts degree in English Literature from Penn State University. She lives in the Catskill Mountain region of New York with her husband, Richard, and their son, Chip. Her interests include reading, reading, and more reading, along with hiking, gardening, visiting museums and historical sites, and sleeping in on Saturday mornings.